Original title:
Breezes Beneath the Palm Trees

Copyright © 2025 Creative Arts Management OÜ
All rights reserved.

Author: Lila Davenport
ISBN HARDBACK: 978-1-80581-630-0
ISBN PAPERBACK: 978-1-80581-157-2
ISBN EBOOK: 978-1-80581-630-0

Echoes of Nature's Gentle Breath

Whispers dance through fronds worn,
As squirrels giggle, nuts adorn.
The breeze teases hats off heads,
While seagulls play leapfrog in spreads.

A lizard flips, a leap ensues,
It's shirtless day, flip-flop news.
The palm leaves wave a funny cheer,
While the sun's grin spreads from ear to ear.

Secret Life Under the Palms

Down below where shadows play,
Crabs wear sunglasses, they sashay.
A turtle sings, off-key, oh dear,
While ants throw parties, full of cheer.

The coconuts roll, they too like fun,
Chasing each other till the day is done.
Parrots debate the latest trend,
Under palms, they dance, twist, and bend.

Caress of the Sea Air

The salty air tickles noses wide,
As jellyfish float, they won't abide.
Waves giggle, crash, and tease the shore,
While kids scream, "More waves! We want more!"

The sand grins back, with shells in tow,
Footprints giggle, "Where'd you go?"
Seagulls jest with popcorn dreams,
While the ocean sways in silly schemes.

The Swaying Symphony

A chorus of laughter fills the scene,
Palm trees sway, like they're on a screen.
Coconuts joke with old flip-flops,
As the sun tosses in wild plops.

The squirrels wave tiny flags of cheer,
While ants parade as if they steer.
The breeze crackles with playful sass,
Turning every moment into a class.

Soliloquy of the Palm Canopy

In the shade, a parrot sings,
Sipping on coconut flings,
Dancing leaves, they twist and twirl,
While the ground squirrels start to whirl.

Sun hats flying, quite a sight,
A lazy rabbit joins the fight,
Chasing shadows, quick and spry,
Until a butterfly zooms by.

With each gust, the palms confide,
Their secrets in a swaying stride,
Laughter echoes, quite absurd,
As crickets chirp, their songs unheard.

Lemonade spills, it's quite the blunder,
While ants march in, a hungry thunder,
Underneath the palm's wide grin,
Life's but a jest, we all join in.

Nature's Secrets in the Softest Touch

Giggling waves, they tickle toes,
Ticklish pelicans strike a pose,
Between the fronds, a wink is seen,
As the lizards plan their routine.

Swaying hearts and silly sighs,
A sunburned bee learns to fly,
While chatty crabs exchange their news,
In the shell of a curious shoe.

Coconuts fall like jokes from trees,
Bouncing off a bumbling breeze,
Seagulls squawk, they've lost their hats,
While iguanas debate with cats.

A hammock hums with playful grace,
As snoozing folks mishandle space,
In this palm-touched, giggly land,
Nature's secrets, oh so grand.

Sunlight Dappled Dreams

The sun does play, it's quite the trick,
With shadows dancing, slick and quick.
A squirrel sneezed, then lost his chew,
The banana peels all shout, "Woohoo!"

A lazy cat sprawls, tongue out wide,
Chasing the warmth, no need to hide.
Long naps ensue on this sunny day,
While the distant goat starts to bray.

A cheeky breeze whispers sweet confessions,
As birds form bands of odd impressions.
A parrot cackles, claims it's grand,
Stealing seeds from the farmer's hand.

Oh laughter spills from coconut shells,
Where secrets hide and humor dwells.
With sunlight dappled on every face,
This island life is a comical place.

Songs of the Tropical Sun

In the morn, the roosters crow,
They sound like tenors, don't you know?
The sun peeks in, it starts to sing,
While ants form lines, doing their thing.

A ukulele strummed by a goat,
Plucking notes, you should take note.
The monkeys join, throw in a beat,
As they dance to the rhythm of their feet.

A turtle has found a sunbathing spot,
But took too long, now it's all hot.
He hops in the sea with a splash and a yawn,
Singing off-key as he strolls at dawn.

In this symphony of tropical cheer,
We laugh at all the quirky here.
With melodies bright and spirits high,
Sunshine's the jam, it'll never die.

Memories in the Shade

Under the leaves where coolness sneaks,
We trade tall tales and laugh for weeks.
A lizard skateboards on palm fronds,
Spinning tricks till the laughter responds.

A picnic spread with fruits aplenty,
A watermelon slice carries more than twenty.
The bees buzz by, with silly pride,
They steal the juice, but we just chide.

A hammock sways with stories told,
Of mermaids found and treasures bold.
But as we nap, a sneeze erupts,
And suddenly the whole scene disrupts.

Memories bloom in the shade's embrace,
Comedic moments we can't replace.
These sunlit hours, forever sweet,
In laughter's arms, we find our seat.

Shifting Patterns in the Breeze

The wind does play like a cheeky sprite,
Knocking off hats in its playful flight.
A parrot shrieks, "Look at my beak!"
The madness unfolds, 'tis quite unique.

Palm leaves rustle, gossiping trees,
Spreading the word of the honey bees.
A crab waltzes past, dressed in flair,
With a jaunty step, like it doesn't care.

A coconut drops with a thunderous clunk,
Startling the dog, who jumps with a funk.
While the iguana shakes its tail,
Watching the world, as it sets sail.

In every gust, a chuckle hides,
Where a squirrel performs as it glides.
With nature's humor sprinkled around,
Life in this place is joyfully unbound.

Delicate Flickers of Life

A lizard in a hurry flies,
Its tail wags like a warning cry.
The sunbeam tickles a balloon,
And sends it dancing, oh what a boon!

Chickens strut with all their might,
They're threading through the golden light.
A cat appears, plotting mischief,
As if the breeze whispers a gift.

Children chase their giggle spree,
While birds eye them, oh what glee!
A squirrel nods with a cheeky grin,
While the lazy dog just rolls, and spins.

Mangoes sway in the gentle sway,
They wear sombreros, just for play.
The whole scene blissfully ponders,
On life's little funny wonders.

Shadows Play Amongst Green Whispers

The shadows dance on warming sand,
While flip-flops lend a helping hand.
A seagull squawks a chuckling tune,
As it steadies on a sandy dune.

A green iguana sneezes loud,
Chasing away a giggling crowd.
Breezy whispers tickle the palm,
Creating an aura of carefree calm.

Kids tumble like marbles in the sun,
Their laughter's loud, oh what fun!
An old parrot mocks a poet's rhyme,
As if he's read it many a time.

Coconuts roll like bowling balls,
While laughter echoes from the stalls.
With each little joy, the day unfolds,
In charming tales that life beholds.

Tales Carried by the Wind

A kite's a fish in the vast blue sea,
It tries to swim, oh so carefree.
With a twist, it flips and dives,
As the wind confirms, it surely thrives.

Laughter floats like candy floss,
On the salty breeze, it comes across.
A crab in slippers scuttles by,
With a flair that makes the seagulls cry.

An octopus dons a pirate's hat,
Pretending to be more than just that.
With jokes that tumble in every wave,
The sea life laughs, wild and brave.

As night descends with twinkling stars,
They wink at tales, told from afar.
The wind whirls tales all around,
Creating joy where laughter is found.

Harmony in Tropical Tranquility

In a hammock, dreams take flight,
Swinging gently, pure delight.
A hummingbird strums a soft tune,
While lizards dance in a bright monsoon.

Toucan sports a vibrant hat,
As if it's part of some chit-chat.
Frogs jump like they're in a race,
With slip-ups that bring smiles to their face.

A pineapple wears a tiny coat,
While sipping juice, it's quite the quote.
Squirrels laugh at a slip of grace,
As they gather nuts at a swift pace.

Underneath, the nature hums,
While the playful joy truly comes.
Each moment, an amusing delight,
Mirthfully shared in soft twilight.

Dreams of the Island Breeze

A coconut fell with a loud thud,
I ducked just in time, what a dud!
The seagulls squawk with such delight,
While I try to hold my hat tight.

The hammock swings, oh what a sight,
But deep in my dreams, I take flight.
A crab sneaks up, he looks so sly,
I laugh and dance, oh my, oh my!

In the sand, I draw a big smile,
But the tide comes in, oh so vile!
My castle's gone, but who's keeping score?
I'll build it up high, then lose it once more.

Is that a fish wearing a tie?
I swear it winked as it swam by.
In this silly place, I find my glee,
Where even the waves laugh along with me.

Conversations with the Island Wind

The wind came whistling through the bay,
It tickled my ears and stole my toupee.
"Hold on tight!" I said with a grin,
Then I lost my hat, and the game did begin.

"Do you think it's funny, dear air?"
I asked the breeze, but it didn't care.
It danced with the leaves, oh what a sight,
While I chased my flip-flops with all my might.

A parrot perched with a cheeky squawk,
Joining the wind in an insane walk.
We laughed at the sun, shining so bold,
Making shadows that wiggle and mold.

"Let's race the waves!" the wind did say,
So we sprinted along, come what may.
With every gust, I felt so free,
Even if my hairstyle was a catastrophe!

Mist and Sunlight in Harmony

The mist rolled in, oh so fluffy,
As I tripped over flip-flops, feeling gruffy.
"Hello!" I laughed at the cloudy foe,
It giggled back, inching down low.

Sunlight peeked, playing hide and seek,
While I fumbled snacks and dropped my cheek.
"Just another day of thongs and soup!"
The garden gnome joined in, doing a loop.

"Are those flowers dancing?" I wondered aloud,
But they stood still, just like the cloud.
My drink spilled over, what a catastrophe,
But the flowers danced, oh, it was a parody!

In the fog, I lost my way,
A lizard winked and started to play.
Mirth and charm wrapped tight like a locket,
Where even the sun wore a colorful jacket!

Paradise's Breath

In paradise, where laughter resides,
I found a crab that wanted to ride.
He pinched my toe and did a jig,
So I joined in, feeling quite big.

The palm trees swayed, doing their dance,
While a tourist tripped in a strange romance.
"I came for peace!" he stumbled and said,
But the beach ball hit him right on the head.

Seagulls swooped low with grand delight,
Stealing my sandwich, oh what a sight.
I shouted "no!" but they didn't care,
Just flying around, with their cheeky flair.

As the sun dipped down, the stars took stage,
I tripped on my towel and fell on the page.
But in this paradise, nothing's a fuss,
Just laughter and joy, and a little bit of rust!

Dreaming Under a Canopy of Stars

When night falls and the sky's a show,
I wrestle with my thoughts, but they won't go.
A twinkling light winks in cheeky glee,
"Stop counting sheep, just check out me!"

The moon rolls its eyes, a smirk on its face,
"Why lie awake? It's a silly race!"
Stars laugh together, a celestial joke,
"Just close those peepers, you sleepy bloke!"

Rhapsody in the Rustling Palms

The palms sway gently, their dance quite absurd,
They gossip about things that have never occurred.
"Do you think he'll show? He said he would come!"
"Last I heard, he's still stuck playing his drum."

A chattering parrot, full of hot air,
Chimes in with tales of a feathery fair.
"Discounted delights, oh what a great night!"
"Let's fill up our mugs and keep the drinks light!"

Caresses of the Gentle Wind

The cool gusts tickle, like an old friend's jest,
"Hey there, sunbather, get out of your nest!
I've got plans to make sandcastles await,
Get a move on already, or it'll be too late!"

The sun shines down, a mischievous troll,
"I bet you can't tell me your favorite role!"
"Catching ice cream as it melts away,"
"Better hurry, there's a drip—hey, no delay!"

Reflections in the Leafy Whisper

Leaves chuckle softly, shades of green delight,
"Why does that squirrel think he's such a sight?
With his fluffy tail and that goofy grin,
He wobbles and tumbles, never knows he can win!"

A distant bark sounds, the dog's in on the fun,
"How many squirrels does it take to outrun?"
"Two thousand!" the leaves rustle with cheer,
As the pup flops down, they share a good leer!

Fragrant Whispers of the Tropics

In the shade, a parrot sings,
While a monkey steals my things.
Coconuts roll like bowling balls,
Falling down on sunny calls.

Sipping juice, I start to sway,
The hammock says 'Let's pause today!'
A breeze tickles my sun-kissed nose,
And the hammock tangoes, it knows!

Laughter dances from tree to tree,
As squirrels plan their next great spree.
A pineapple wears a silly hat,
And I can't help but laugh at that!

The sun dips low, don't shed a tear,
Tomorrow brings more fun right here.
In this place of giggles and cheer,
I'll continue chasing joy, my dear!

Chasing Sunlight through the Grove

Sunlight flickers as I dash,
Past a lizard with a splash.
Racing shadows on the ground,
Who will win? Not sure—profound!

Bananas swing like monkeys do,
I wobble like a ball of glue.
Laughter winks through leaves above,
This silly chase I dearly love!

Twirling hats and playful pranks,
The squirrels form their own cool ranks.
A farting frog hops by with glee,
"Excuse me!" he croaks, "That's just me!"

As the sun finally lays to rest,
I've chased my joy; I've surely blessed.
Tomorrow I'll return again,
To dance with shadows, laugh, and grin!

Shades of Solitude

In my spot beneath the trees,
I sip cold drinks and feel the breeze.
The grass tickles my bare feet,
While crickets play a tuneful beat.

A wise old owl looks down and grins,
"What's up, my friend? Have you seen my twins?"
I chuckle at the tale he spins,
As laughter echoes through the winds.

A turtle dreams of a racing game,
With shadows racing, quite the fame.
A beetle struts with such flair and pride,
Proudly claiming the leaf as his ride.

As twilight deepens, I find my cheer,
Filled with dreams that draw me near.
In my corner of joy and fun,
In silence, I'm anything but done!

Ebb and Flow of Rustling Palms

The palms sway like they're in a dance,
While squirrels take the chance to prance.
Fluffy clouds aim for the race,
Chasing shadows with playful grace.

A crab is plotting in the sand,
Dreaming of his rock band.
Drumsticks made from seashell loot,
But they scoot away—now that's cute!

My sandwich flies away, oh dear!
A seagull claims it, filled with cheer.
With laughter, I reclaim my peace,
While the seabreeze grants me sweet release.

As the stars peek through, I sigh,
Under twinkling lights, I dream and lie.
In this silly circus of delight,
My heart dances through the night!

Murmurs of the Coastal Air

Seagulls squawk, they think they're wise,
But they steal fries right before our eyes.
Waves roll in, a slippery show,
And someone falls, a comical blow.

Cool winds blow, hats take flight,
Chasing them down, what a sight!
Children giggle, sand in their hair,
While adults complain, 'Life's not fair!'

Beach balls bounce with a loud thud,
Someone trips, falls face first in the mud.
Sunscreen slathered like frosting thick,
A sticky mess, what a silly trick!

After the fun, the day fades slow,
Sunset painted in a brilliant glow.
With laughter echoing on the shore,
We grin and joke, and then we roar!

Embrace of the Summer Zephyr

A gentle tickle, the wind's so sly,
It sends my hat into the sky.
Chasing it down, we laugh and scream,
As it lands in someone's ice cream!

Tanned legs stretch, umbrellas flip,
Sandcastle dreams go for a trip.
A toddler grins with a mischievous face,
As he buries dad in a sandy embrace.

Cool drinks spill as we leap for joy,
After a splash from that silly boy.
Seashells collected, but most are lost,
In the laughter, we've paid the cost.

As the sun dips low, shadows play,
Funny memories linger, bright as day.
With tanned skin and goofy grins,
We plan next year to do it again!

Tides of Tranquility

The tide rolls in, a slippery game,
We're dodging waves, it's never the same.
Someone slips, and down they go,
With a splash and a laugh, they're put on show!

Drinks in hand, we try to chill,
But a seagull swoops for a quick thrill.
Stealing snacks like it's a grand heist,
We laugh at the bandit, oh so precise!

Sun hats peek from behind the sand,
As friends create castles, looking grand.
But the tide's a trickster, no doubt at all,
Soon it washes away every wall!

But when the sun sets, we share a cheer,
For the silly moments that bring us near.
With tales to tell, we pack up and sway,
Laughing together, we end the day!

Celestial Dances Among the Palms

Under palms swaying, we dance about,
Dodging coconuts, without a doubt!
Someone yells, 'Watch out!' as they fall,
In this tropical breeze, we're having a ball!

Friends all gather with drinks so bright,
Each one claims, 'Mine's the best tonight!'
But with a mix-up, we take a sip,
And suddenly find ourselves on a trip!

Laughter rings through the sunny haze,
With sandy toes and hapless ways.
Who's got the towel? Oh wait, that's mine!
Wrapped up like burritos, feeling just fine!

As stars twinkle and we close our eyes,
We dream of paths where laughter lies.
With palm trees swaying, life's a delight,
We dance through the night, oh what a sight!

The Heartbeat of Island Air

Waves tickle sand with a playful spell,
Seagulls squawk like they know it well.
Palm fronds dance, waving hello,
As I trip on the roots—oh no, oh no!

Coconuts clatter, what a surprise,
One drops down right between my eyes!
Laughing hats fly, it's quite the show,
Nature's circus, it steals the glow!

Sunshine races, a game to play,
Chasing shadows that run away.
With each giggle, the warmth does stay,
Island air—what a zany day!

Catch the giggles, let spirits rise,
Even the lizards wear comical ties.
In the rhythm of fun, we lose all care,
Heartbeat smiles in the sunny air!

Conversations with the Sun

The sun winks cheekily, throwing heat,
"I'll bake your cookies, you fetch the seat!"
Clouds gossip petty, full of mirth,
As I sip coconuts, they plot my dearth.

Sandy toes dancing, shoes in retreat,
"We'll tan until the day's bittersweet."
The sun chuckles, "Don't burn too much!
Add a little wiggle, feel the touch!"

Waves join in, echoing the fun,
"Splash here and there, we'll be number one!"
A dolphin jumps, showing off his spin,
While I'm flopping like a fish—oh, win!

Whispers of laughter, floating on air,
Every sunbeam, a party to share.
Even the crabs think life is grand,
Talking with the sun—now isn't it planned?

Melody of the Lush Retreat

Leaves clink together, a musical chime,
While monkeys gossip—they're quite sublime.
Rapscallion rabbits hop to the beat,
Dancing around my unsuspecting feet!

Laughter elopes in the twinkling light,
As fireflies join in, a winking sight.
The breeze hums tunes of forgotten lore,
While I skedaddle, cracking up on the floor!

Waterfalls giggle, splashing in glee,
Jellyfish sing songs from the deep sea.
A parrot squawks, adding flair to the beat,
In this lush retreat, life feels so sweet!

The shadows shimmy on vibrant green,
A hilarious dance, too funny to mean.
With every chuckle, the night takes flight,
In this melody, pure joy feels right!

Canvas of Shadows and Light

Dappled sunlight paints a silly scene,
While I trip over vines, looking quite keen.
Swaying shadows whisper a tale,
Of a squirrel in shades, swish and flail!

Painted laughter splashes on the ground,
As critters rally, a brigade profound.
Palms sway elegantly, with hands on hips,
Teasing little lizards, with clumsy slips!

Sunset giggles, splashing colors bright,
As I juggle seashells in fading light.
The ocean joins in, waves full of jest,
Who knew the sunset could be such a fest?

Canvas of fun, with splatters of cheer,
Even the clowns get a big round of jeer.
So let your shadows find rhythm and rhyme,
In this wild world, we dance out of time!

Whirl of the Timid Breeze

A gentle whoosh, a soft delight,
Dancing leaves in the fading light.
A scared little gust, it makes me grin,
Trying to enter, but just can't get in.

Whirling around like a playful cat,
Tickling toes, oh, look at that!
It sways the fronds, oh what a tease,
Hiding its strength like an awkward sneeze.

Lush Canopy Conversations

The palm trees gossip, oh what a sight,
Whispering jokes about a bird's flight.
"Did you hear Timmy tripped on the sand?
Fell flat on his face, isn't life grand?"

With rustling laughter, they wave along,
Sharing the secrets of sun and song.
Dancing their tales, they shake and sway,
While turtles below just snicker and play.

My Solace in Swirling Green

In a world of green, my worries fade,
Chasing a lizard, though I'm afraid.
He jumps and zips, just look at him go,
While I trip over roots, in quite a show.

With shades of emerald, it's quiet and bright,
A hammock swings gently, what pure delight.
But here comes the breeze, and oh what a jest!
It sways my rest with a chuckle, no rest!

Tropical Tides of Tranquility

The tides are playing a tune so sweet,
Like a beachy rhythm beneath my feet.
Palm trees dance in a quirky groove,
Trying to show me how to move.

With every wave, my worries flee,
It's a slapstick scene, come laugh with me!
A shell rolls by with a giggle and grin,
In this silly paradise, let the fun begin!

Napping in the Embrace of Leaves

The sun's a lazy cat on high,
While I snooze beneath the sky.
A leaf falls down, it tickles my nose,
Awake! I shout, like a startled rose.

The wind plays tricks with my hat,
Sailing away—what's up with that?
I chase it down, like a wild, lost sheep,
But all I find is a nap to keep.

The palms look down, they laugh and sway,
As I fumble and stumble in my play.
They whisper secrets, but I just yawn,
Still dreaming of breakfast, please don't be gone!

So here I lie, in nature's quilt,
With giggles danced through sunbeams spilt.
Who needs a bed when leaves are around?
In this silly world, fun is abound!

Huahine's Silent Song

In Huahine, the sea takes a nap,
While I sit, waiting for a crabby chap.
He wanders by, with claws held high,
Looks at me as if to say, 'Why?'

The waves chuckle, a rhythmic tease,
As I swat flies, not feeling at ease.
A parrot squawks a joke so grand,
But all I catch is the grain of sand.

The trees, they whisper, 'Psst, over here!'
But I'm too busy, indulging my beer.
Sunburned and laughing at shadows that chase,
I dance with delight, in this whimsical place.

And though they sing a silent tune,
I laugh aloud, beneath the moon.
In Huahine, life's a silly jest,
Where even the crabs seem to have a quest!

Twilight among the Fronds

Twilight drapes in colors bright,
As I trip over roots, what a sight!
The fronds are swaying with gentle glee,
While I wonder if they laugh at me.

A firefly winks, 'Come join the dance!'
But I trip again, not given a chance.
The sky dons purple, orange, and pink,
While I consider another drink.

The shadows giggle, oh what a tease,
As I twirl and stumble, down on my knees.
The palms all sigh, 'It's getting late,'
While I try to juggle, but just consolidate.

In twilight's embrace, I laugh and fall,
With fronds all around, I heed their call.
Tomorrow I'll plan, or maybe just sway,
In this funny tale of evening's play.

Reflections in Shimmering Shadows

Under the palms, the shadows roam,
Mirroring giggles like a mobile home.
I see my reflection, looking quite merry,
But my hat flew off, like a little fairy.

The ocean laughs, with a wave and a splish,
As I search for my hat, that I almost miss.
Then a dolphin peeks, with a cheeky grin,
Like, 'Good luck with that!'—where to begin?

The flip-flops dance, they're mocking my stride,
As I bump and wiggle, with glee I abide.
With palms as witnesses to my plight,
I giggle at shadows in fading light.

So let them shimmer, these silly glows,
While I chase my hat where the river flows.
In the land of the quirky, let laughter ring,
With reflections of joy in the silly spring.

Heartbeats of the Island Wind

In the shade, a coconut drops,
A clumsy bird, it takes a flop.
The monkeys giggle from the tree,
Who knew fruit was so slippery?

Sandy toes and sun-kissed skin,
A crab pinches—let the games begin!
We'd chase the waves, no time to pout,
Until a wave waved back, no doubt!

A parrot squawks, he sings off-key,
He thinks he's great—oh, let him be!
With lemonade, we cheers once more,
The ice just fled, right to the shore.

Beneath the palms, we strut and sway,
In this funny dance, we lose our way.
Pinch my cheek, laugh hard, and shout,
For on this isle, we twist about!

Solace Among the Green Canopy

The ferns play hide and seek today,
While lizards laugh and run away.
A picnic flop—a sandwich flies,
But hey, it's lunch for hungry fries!

Grasshoppers join our merry jam,
With tiny beats, they go 'bam-bam!'
A squirrel's acorn hits my head,
And now I'm feeling nutty, instead!

The breeze spills tea with pure delight,
As ants march past in straight, neat lines.
But where's the sugar? Oh, the strife!
Guess we'll have salty bugs for life!

Up in the trees, we let out shrieks,
With birdy dreams and jungle leaks.
We'll laugh as leaves come tumbling down,
In this canopy, we're the crowned clowns!

Embracing the Hushed Jungle

In the hush, a loud frog croaks,
Turns out he's got some wild jokes.
A rustle here, a giggle there,
Creatures chuckle without a care.

A sloth slides down, oh so slow,
He's king of chill, don't you know?
With a grin, he gives a wave,
Like, hurry up! Just misbehave!

The vines twist in a silly dance,
While owls wonder, 'What's with the prance?'
A firefly blinks—oh, what a show!
Just don't trip over your toe, oh no!

In leafy shades, laughter rings,
Where nothing's serious, just funny things.
With butterflies as our giggling crew,
We'll dance 'til twilight welcomes you!

Secrets in the Fronded Light

Underneath these leafy lights,
I found a snail with dreams of flights.
He said, 'I'll glide—make no mistake!'
But all he did was take a break.

In shadows small, a beetle pranced,
He boogied hard, not even chanced.
But oh dear friend, your dance is slick,
I can't breathe, you made me tick!

The sunbeams wink, they tease the ground,
As curious critters gather round.
Confetti leaves come down like rain,
And suddenly, we're all insane!

In the whispers, tales are spun,
Of secret nights and burning sun.
With laughter high, we spin and glide,
In secret worlds where giggles reside!

Transitory Dance of Shadows

In the shade where shadows play,
Laughter dances day by day.
A startled squirrel takes a leap,
While sunbeams promise not to creep.

The sandcastles start to sway,
As waves pull giggles far away.
A crab in sunglasses struts around,
His sideways shuffle quite profound.

Frisbees fly, and so do dreams,
As seagulls plot in crafty schemes.
With sunburned noses, we all grin,
A summer jest that makes us spin.

But shadows grow as daylight wanes,
While ocean whispers tickle brains.
We find our homes beneath the stars,
Counting laughter, not the scars.

The Rhythm of Whispering Palms

The palms do sway to tunes unheard,
As if they've danced to every word.
A coconut drops, a comical thud,
While tourists jump in panic-flood.

With flip-flops flapping like a bird,
They chase a ball without a word.
The sunburned lobster cries, "Oh dear!"
As waves crash down—it's slapstick cheer!

A toucan tries to steal a fry,
While giggling kids just wonder why.
The seagulls caw a raucous sound,
As peanut snacks fly all around.

The dusk brings tales of blunders bright,
Sand in our shoes, oh what a sight.
We dance with laughter, hand in hand,
Embracing joy across the sand.

Woven Tales of Coastal Calm

On sandy shores where stories weave,
The gossip of the ocean leaves.
Shells tell tales of fish that prank,
While kids all giggle at the tank.

A dog digs furiously for treasure,
Each found stick brings a newfound pleasure.
The ice cream truck, a distant horn,
Spills sticky tales of summer's dawn.

Kites are tangled in a curious vine,
Parents sigh, "Again? Just one more time!"
While beach balls bounce on giggling heads,
And whose is whose? No one dreads.

With salty hair and laughter loud,
We build our dreams, all packed in a cloud.
As dusk descends, our stories blend,
In every wave, a message penned.

Islands in the Whispering Wind

In islands where the wind's a friend,
Hammocks sway, but naps don't tend.
A parrot laughs as sailors stumble,
Around their toes, the coconuts tumble.

The breeze invents new hairstyles wild,
With every gust, I'm just a child.
A crab with swagger, proud and spry,
Tips his hat as I walk by.

Pirates in flip-flops, what a sight,
Claiming treasure with no fright.
The sun dips low, a radiant glow,
And laughter echoes, steals the show!

As stars peek out, the tales are spun,
With every wave, the joy's begun.
On islands kissed by gentle air,
We find the magic everywhere.

Whispers of the Wind

A parrot squawks with all its might,
The monkeys chatter, what a sight!
Coconuts fall, it's quite the scene,
Who knew a palm could be so mean?

Dancing leaves that tickle my nose,
An iguana strikes a funny pose!
The wind plays hide and seek with me,
Oh what fun this tropical spree!

The sun's a jokester, bold and bright,
Turning midday into pure delight.
The sand too hot, I jump and squeal,
Next time, socks! That's my deal!

In this paradise of playful glee,
Every breeze whispers, "Come and see!"
Laughter floats on each swirling gust,
In this mirthful place, I trust!

Shadows of Serenity

Under palms where shadows play,
I tripped on roots, oh what a day!
Sand to my toes, I try to stand,
The lizard laughs, it outsmarts my hand.

A crab scuttles with a funny gait,
While I struggle to coordinate.
Is this serenity or a jest?
The ocean joins in, it knows best!

The twilight dims, a starfish grins,
I dance around trying to win.
With goofy moves, I sway and flail,
A dolphin laughs, it's a funny tale!

In shadows deep, we share a jest,
Nature laughs, it's truly blessed.
Underneath the moon's soft sheen,
We are all part of this funny scene!

Dance of the Tropical Leaves

Leaves waltz together in delight,
A sloth joins in, what a sight!
He really thinks he's got the groove,
But he's just hanging, trying to move!

Swaying to tunes of the breeze,
Bumbling bees buzzing with ease.
"Why don't you join?" they seem to buzz,
I say, "Hold on, wait! What's the fuss?"

A gecko slides in with a grin,
Lost his rhythm but found his chin.
Laughter echoes through the air,
Who knew dancing would cause despair?

Yet under the palms, we all unite,
In this goofy twilight, such a sight.
With every mishap, joy appears,
Life's a dance that's filled with cheers!

Echoes of Ocean Sighs

The waves whisper secrets, oh so sly,
They giggle softly, "Come on, try!"
I attempt to surf but fall instead,
A fish chuckles, "Sleep in your bed!"

Seagulls cackle on the shore,
As I chase them more and more.
They flap away, laughing with glee,
What a day for a wannabe!

The tide rolls in with a playful pout,
"Can't catch me!" it seems to shout.
No way to win in this delightful game,
But I'll keep laughing, that's my claim!

In echoes of laughter by the sea,
Nature keeps dishing fun for free.
So here I stay, with sand and sighs,
In a world where joy never dies!

A Serenade for Swaying Silhouettes

The palms dance in silly grace,
As squirrels in tuxedos romp and race.
A coconut rolls down with a clunk,
While a parrot pretends to be the funk.

Laughter bounces like a beach ball high,
While crabs clink their claws, giving a sigh.
The sun winks at the moon with a laugh,
And dances along like a playful calf.

Gentle whisperings tickle the leaves,
As geckos play peek-a-boo, or so it seems.
They chat in secret, in code and rhyme,
While bees nap around, sipping the thyme.

With every gust, the party grows bold,
As shells share tales of adventures told.
The world spins round like a merry-go,
Where even the sandcastles dance to and fro.

Twilight's Caress on Green Foliage

At dusk, the shadows begin to prance,
As fireflies start their glowing dance.
A raccoon stumbles, tripping on flair,
While owls critique with a curious stare.

The sky blushes like a bashful teen,
As clouds gossip, if you know what I mean.
The stars roll their eyes, throwing sparkles around,
While night crickets chirp without making a sound.

A breeze swoops in, tickling each nose,
As a turtle chuckles, his shell full of prose.
Laughter floats softly on the night air,
With echoes of giggles, no burdens to bear.

In the dusky light, mischief does thrive,
With shadows dancing, feeling alive.
The moon's giggle hides in its glow,
While nighttime revelers steal the show.

Harmonies in the Island Breeze

The wind hums tunes through palm fronds high,
As monkeys drum on coconuts nearby.
A goat wears glasses, looking quite sly,
While the sun grins wide in the deep blue sky.

Kites in the air, making loops and dive,
As children chase them, feeling so alive.
A crab with a hat shows off its style,
Making shells giggle and wink with a smile.

The rhythm of rustling leaves and waves,
Whispers the secrets that nature saves.
Every gust plays a game of tag,
While frogs croak loudly, never a drag.

In this chatty place where the wild things roam,
Even the fish know how to feel at home.
They splash around, making ripples of cheer,
While every creature finds friendship here.

Gossamer Touch of Nature's Breath

A slight puff of air brings tales of old,
Where ants wear capes, feeling quite bold.
Lizards high-five as winds take a twirl,
With a laugh, they lose their tails, oh what a whirl!

The sun sneezes glitter, takes a break,
While flowers giggle, shaking awake.
Bees buzz a tune, playing sax on a stem,
While mice write songs, all out on a whim.

The clouds wear jackets, all puffy and bright,
While the windy breeze joins in for the night.
A chorus of creatures, both big and small,
Singing together, they're having a ball.

With every flap, and flutter they show,
That nature's a stage with a colorful glow.
So join in the fun, sway along in delight,
For laughter and joy make everything bright.

Murmurs Along Shaded Paths

Underneath the leafy groves,
Squirrels dance on tiny toes.
Whispers float from branches high,
Telling tales of the birds that fly.

The lizards sunbathe with a grin,
Debating who could be the king.
While bugs in suits debate their fate,
In a boardroom made of a giant plate.

Monkeys swing with laughter loud,
Waving wildly, feeling proud.
They tease the breeze, play hide and seek,
Making the palm fronds sway and creak.

So join us here with laughter free,
In the shade of the verdant tree.
Where nature's humor we embrace,
And share a smile in this green space.

The Calm of Canopy Caresses

In the shade, a dip is found,
Where the grass is soft and round.
Picnic ants march with a plan,
Stealing crumbs from every man.

Kites get tangled in the leaves,
As children giggle, pulling sleeves.
With the wind, they take a flight,
Dreaming stars in broad daylight.

A coconut rolls, a seagull swoops,
The tide decides to join the Troops.
Nature laughs with a playful sound,
As laughter echoes all around.

So we lounge under skies so blue,
With sun hats and a drink or two.
Let's relish this calm parade,
Underneath the leafy shade.

Essence of the Sun-kissed Isles

Coconut drinks with little umbrellas,
Wobbly tables, and old propellers.
Lime pies dance on sunlit slabs,
While tourists chase their flapping flaps.

The sun's bright hat is tipped just right,
As crabs perform their wiggly fight.
Seagulls squawk like they own the place,
While fish laugh, splashing with grace.

Lazy palms sigh in the heat,
As flip-flops shuffle with happy feet.
A turtle rolls on a sun-soaked rock,
While pelicans check their last TikTok.

In this haven with laughable sights,
We embrace the day and its silly flights.
Join in the mirth of island glee,
As we find mischief 'neath each tree.

Nature's Gentle Lullaby

Crickets chirp in syncopation,
Setting up a wild celebration.
Fireflies twinkle with a wink,
As nature plots and plans to drink.

A raccoon wearing a tiny hat,
Steals a snack from the garden mat.
While frogs croak tunes with silly sync,
Jumping high, they make us think.

There's a breeze that tickles the skin,
And whispers secrets of where to begin.
The stars join in for a midnight show,
As the night sky glows in soft flow.

So let the laughter fill the air,
In this wild setting without a care.
For the night is young, and dreams run free,
As we rock to nature's soft melody.

Gentle Currents in the Canopy

The leaves are all a-flutter, so light,
A squirrel trips and loses his sight.
With a whoops and a holler, he spins around,
Chasing shadows, he leaps and he's down.

The flowers giggle in bright summer glee,
As ants dance a jig, oh so carefree.
Whispers of mischief in each gentle gust,
Even the pollen joins in, it must!

A lizard struts, with a flair for the scene,
He winks at a butterfly, oh what a dream!
But he forgets his next move: a slip and a slide,
Into a puddle, how he splashed wide!

In this playful world of light-hearted cheer,
Every rustle and chuckle we happily hear.
So gather your laughter, let joy make its way,
Under the canopy, let's dance and let play!

Secrets of Sunlit Shade

In the shade where the dappled light plays,
A crabby old turtle complains for days.
He shouts at the sun, 'Oh, why so bright?
Can't you see I'm trying to nap in this light?'

Meanwhile, the shadows just chuckle and tease,
As they play tag with the cool summer breeze.
A rabbit hops by, wearing sunglasses bold,
While ants throw a party, with stories retold.

A grasshopper sings, he's got rhythm and flair,
He's got all of the critters just dancing with care.
Even the breeze joins with a gentle sway,
As secrets unfold in the warm light of day.

So gather around, where the sunlight is bright,
With laughter and songs, we dance with delight.
Here in our haven, we'll share all our tales,
Under sunlit shade, where mirth never fails!

Laughter of the Ferns

In the garden of ferns, it's a festive day,
When a caterpillar slips, in an awkward ballet.
He wiggles and jiggled, trying to impress,
But ends up in a puddle, oh what a mess!

The ferns giggle softly, they rustle and sway,
As the beetles all gather to join in the play.
One beetle declares, 'I've got moves like a star!'
But trips over roots, now he's near a jar!

A ladybug chimes in, 'Hold steady my friend,
Let's join in the fun, this giggle won't end.'
With a flick of their wings, they take to the air,
And laugh at the world without a single care.

From morning till evening, the laughter shall ring,
With the joy of the ferns, oh what joy they bring.
In every green corner, their secrets unfold,
As they whisper and chuckle, their stories retold!

A Symphony of Swaying Fronds

The rhythm of palm leaves is a fanciful tune,
As a raccoon jigs under the watchful moon.
His dance is a sight, so wild and so free,
With a tail that's a drum, oh listen to me!

A parrot joins in, with feathers so bright,
She squawks a sweet song, what a marvelous flight!
While the wind plays the flute, with soft, gentle sighs,
The ferns clap along, oh what a surprise!

The crickets compose, with their fiddles and bows,
As the daisies tap feet, in their tiny little rows.
With every soft rustle, the laughter expands,
In this symphony grand, let's all join hands!

So sway with the fronds, let your joy intertwine,
In this orchestra of nature, with moments divine.
Underneath the stars, our hearts will take flight,
As we dance to the music of the magical night!

Murmurs of a Forgotten Paradise

In the shade of leafy giants,
Squirrels plot an acorn heist,
While lazy lizards sunbathe,
And dream of being very nice.

Chickens strut with fancy flair,
Clucking gossip, bold and bright,
As tropical fish swim by,
In search of a dazzling bite.

Coconuts drop with a thunk,
A monkey steals my fruity drink,
While I'll just laugh and say,
Life's a joke, what do you think?

So here we laugh with joy,
In this land of sunlit glee,
Where the wild and wacky roam,
And play charades by the sea.

Secrets of Sun-soaked Serenity

Waves whisper secrets with a splash,
As crabs dance a silly jig,
Turtles make a daring dash,
To keep up with a two-legged gig.

The sun wears a goofy grin,
As it starts to spill some tea,
Telling tales of mischief's win,
And a wibbly, wobbly bee.

Parrots squawk in vibrant tones,
Joining in the sunny prank,
While the wind just snores and moans,
And steals the hat from a crank.

In this land of hilarious sights,
Joy hangs in the palm leaves high,
With each chuckle, we take flight,
Beneath a giggling sky.

The Comfort of Verdant Dreams

Underneath the leafy green,
Lies a chair for a dozing cat,
While the sun's all warm and keen,
    On a nap that's soft and fat.

Lizards dance in silly shoes,
Doing the cha-cha with a twist,
All while I chuckle and muse,
    About life's uncanny list.

Coconut juice spills with a plop,
    As the tropics sing a tune,
And the shadows start to bop,
    In the cozy afternoon.

With laughter drifting on warm air,
And mischief lurking near the sea,
    I find joy beyond compare,
    In this land of happy glee.

A Haven of Gentle Winds

A breeze tickles through the fronds,
As I spy a startled hare,
Chasing butterflies it responds,
With a hop and twist of flair.

Charming critters make a scene,
With antics wild and free,
Like a clown in a big green bean,
Jumping high just to tease me.

Palm leaves share their silly tales,
To the rhythm of the sea,
While I sip on fruit-filled pails,
Wondering who'll join the spree.

So come and join this wacky place,
Where laughter fills the air,
In every corner, there's a chase,
As joy becomes our main affair.

Island Air and Daydreams

The parrot yells, 'What's the plan?'
Everyone laughs, sipping from a can.
A coconut falls like a runaway truck,
We dodge and giggle, oh what luck!

The hammock sways, it starts to creak,
A friend shouts, 'Can you hear that sneak?'
A crab trots by, with no sense of shame,
He struts around, playing his game.

Sunshine dances on our sunburnt skin,
We toast a drink, let the fun begin.
A neighbor snores, lost in sweet dreams,
While we craft jokes more ridiculous than they seem.

In this isle where troubles drift away,
Everyone's a comedian, come what may.
With laughter ringing, we weave the tale,
As palm fronds sway in the vibrant gale.

The Quietude of Canopy Life

Under the leaves, it's peaceful and bright,
A squirrel's antics are quite the sight.
He fights with a fruit, his fierce little prize,
As we munch popcorn, full of surprise.

A lizard struts, like he owns the place,
Hissing at sunshine with style and grace.
He blinks at us, then starts to yawn,
As we laugh, 'Dude, it's a sleepy dawn!'

The shadows tickle and tease our feet,
As we tell stories, both silly and sweet.
A sudden thump, oops, there goes my drink,
Laughter erupts, oh, what do you think?

The world slows down in this leafy cocoon,
As goofy moments rise with the moon.
In this quietude, we're never alone,
As laughter echoes, the best kind of tone.

Encounters with the Gentle Zephyr

Whispers of wind flirt with my hair,
A pig joins in, with a curious stare.
He snorts a greeting, oh what a show,
Pigs can dance too, just so you know!

Floating by, the clouds form a smile,
Waves of laughter, enriching the style.
A seagull swoops down, what a grand thief,
Stealing our chips, oh what disbelief!

The shadows play tag, they spin and twirl,
As I trip over my own dang curl.
With every twist and turn, we burst into fits,
Adding to laughter, the best of the bits.

In the arms of the breeze, we sway to the beat,
Where silliness grows, it can't be beat.
Surrounded by nature, never a bore,
Life is a joke we can't help but adore.

Sunlit Pathways Through the Leaves

On this trail where the sunlight drops,
We skip like kids, having giggly hops.
A stray dog joins, thinks he's part of the crew,
What a sight, with his paw prints askew!

A butterfly flutters, acting all grand,
While I roll my eyes, it won't understand.
'Look at me!' it shouts, doing its dance,
We cheer and laugh, go on, take a chance!

In the dappled light, the fruit seems ripe,
We take a bite, let out a hype!
A friend spits seeds, blasting through the air,
We laugh till we snort, without a care.

With each step forward, the humor grows,
In sunlit pathways, we strike a pose.
The day may fade, but the fun stays bright,
We carry this joy into the night.

The Poetry of Nature's Breath.

In a world where leaves all dance,
They twirl and spin, with giddy glance.
A coconut drops, with a thud!
Who knew that palms were such a dud?

Each rustle brings a giggle near,
Those insects buzzing, oh so sheer.
A squirrel lost his little hat,
He blames the wind; how rude is that!

Whispers of the Canopy

The trees gossip high above,
In their shady club, they shove.
"Who wore that trunk?" they chuckle bright,
And shade the sun from out of sight.

A parrot hoots, on a branch tight,
Announcing jokes in sheer delight.
But all the jokes are utterly stale,
For laughter's light must ride the gale.

Shadows on Sunlit Sands

On the beach, where shadows play,
Sandy feet scamper, come what may.
A crab with swagger, walks on by,
Waving pincers like a tiny guy.

Seagulls swoop with a honking sound,
Stealing chips from where they're found.
The ocean whispers a salty pun,
"Catch me if you can, just for fun!"

Dance of the Swaying Fronds

The fronds do tango in the air,
One slips and falls, but does not care.
With floppy hats, they spin so bold,
Each moment filled with laughter gold.

Underneath their leafy might,
Frogs jump high, a comical sight.
They croak a tune, a ribbit song,
Nature's laughter, where we belong.

www.ingramcontent.com/pod-product-compliance
Lightning Source LLC
Chambersburg PA
CBHW072133070526

4458SCB00016B/1663